WHY JOHNNY CAN'T PUTT...

Jack Ohman

A FIRESIDE BOOK
Published by Simon & Schuster
NEW YORK   LONDON   TORONTO   SYDNEY   TOKYO   SINGAPORE

FIRESIDE
Rockefeller Center
1230 Avenue of the Americas
New York, New York 10020

Manufactured in the United States of America

10   9   8   7   6   5   4   3   2   1

Library of Congress Cataloging-in-Publication Data is available.

ISBN: 0-671-87298-2

ACKNOWLEDGMENTS

Golf, unfortunately, is not my game. I don't know, exactly, what my game *is* or if I will ever have a game at which I can excel. But that doesn't stop me from golfing. Perhaps it's an obsessive-compulsive disorder.

I enjoy golf, however. I began golfing when I was 14 years old, which, at this writing, was about 20 years ago. Craig Mohn, Tim Cushing, Mark Opsahl, and I golfed at a little par-three course back in Roseville, Minnesota. None of the aforementioned golfers has, as yet, made the PGA Tour, but we were quite the foursome with old garage-sale clubs, plaid bags, and three-for-a-buck golf balls. Even then, golf cut into what little disposable income I had available. That hasn't changed.

There are many people with whom I have golfed over the years. I have done the most golfing with my brother-in-law David Dunham, who claims to have hit a golf ball 320 yards. I once saw him hit a golf ball so hard my teeth hurt, so he probably wasn't lying, but this is golf, and golfers are allowed some exaggeration. It's in the USGA Rules of Golf under Rule 37-A, "Golfing Hyperbole."

Now I golf with Bob Hastings, who seems a little pouty if he shoots over 80, and Jim "Floater" Leinfelter, who, having grown up in Minnesota, is expert at chipping out of snow drifts. Winter rules, I guess. My neighbor Steve Birkel is also a golf buddy, although I have spent hours attempting to convince him to give up the game while he still has the chance. Also Ken and Sandy Tweedt, who seem to golf a bit too much, actually. But Ken is a doctor, and the physician's golf prowess is now a part of the Hippocratic Oath. David Judson and Stu Forstrom also have heard me swear uncontrollably on the links. Jeff "Linkster" Gilbertson has contributed greatly to my golfing vocabulary but not to my game.

I gratefully acknowledge the editing talents of my wife, Jan, who has never picked up a club but has picked up many typos, transpositions, transitional errors, and bizarre breaches of taste. She hasn't nailed the gratuitous alliteration, however. My agent, Jeanne Hanson, flogged this book mercilessly with good humor and solid Minnesota sense. I thank her. My editor, Ed Walters, has remained calm throughout all this, and gets a gold star.

Jack Ohman
Portland, Oregon
March 30, 1993

TO JULIA, MY WONDERFUL DAUGHTER

Starting to Golf

Making the decision to start golfing is probably not unlike the decision to start smoking. You probably did it under some sort of duress or drunken stupor or perhaps out of a desire to appear "cool." Maybe it was even peer pressure. It gave you something to do with your hands, to avoid having opposable thumbs for no good reason. And like smoking, it becomes an addiction. You do it because you just, by God, have to do it, and you don't even understand why. Beginning to golf just isn't a rational decision, but there you are.

Most people start golfing because they have alleged friends who golf. More likely, these friends are actually people who happen to be coworkers who golf. My neighbor, for example, told me he wanted to learn to golf because "everybody at work golfs." What a silly reason. I told him to quit his job and find a place where everybody fly-fished. He didn't listen.

I thought he had forgotten about golfing after a while. I would come home from golfing—usually after shooting a spectacularly high score and actually injuring myself through sheer ineptitude—and I would see my neighbor staring at me from his window, wistfully thinking that I had probably had a great time.

Then his wife called me. "Steve wants to learn to golf," she said. "And I really think," she confided, "that he needs to have a relaxing hobby." A long pause.

"Taking drugs is a relaxing hobby. Golf is not a relaxing hobby," I said, trying to discourage her line of reasoning.

She pressed on. I parried, thrusted, and otherwise did everything I could do to protect my neighbor from golf. Finally, I relented and helped pick out a set of clubs for the poor guy. Now, he's more stressed out than ever.

He's got golf to worry about.

Your Course of Action

You should, as a golf consumer (or consumed, actually), be prepared to analyze the various types of golf courses available to you. Be aware that, unfortunately, there is a direct socioeconomic correlation between the golf course you will play on and your annual level of income. Hey, welcome to the global economy. The Republicans who started the game as we know it planned it that way. You'll get used to it.

INCOME:

0 to $20,000 per year: You'll be playing on one of the many fine municipal public courses made possible by the sporting largess of the political power structure, who all play on private courses. Your tax money is also involved here.

Municipal public courses have the following indelible characteristics:

1. Massive piles of broken wooden tees in front of every tee. These are never swept up, but are left as some sort of bizarre prearchaeological statement by the grounds crew.

2. Groups of about 200 people at the first tee. These people may seem to be waiting to golf, but they're actually there to critique your first drive. They tend to specialize in little clucking noises or perhaps low groans, bizarre trilling whistles, and helpful coaching statements, such as "*You duh man,*" or "Nice shot, dipshit."

3. Large brown expanses of dead grass. At first, big patches of dead grass could seem to be simple lack of care. But the municipal public golf courses are run by highly trained public sector employees who want to serve you better and to improve your golf game. Have you ever noticed how much farther a golf ball will roll on dead grass? It's there as part of a deliberate policy to increase your drive distances from 20 up to 150 extra yards. And they say big government doesn't care.

4. Greens with lumpy dead grass over previously existent holes. Again, this may seem to be a case of simple slovenliness, but these dead grass marks are helpful *distance markers* to assist you in judging how hard to tap the putt. Another public service.

5. Unusually slow-moving foursomes. The

municipal public course is perhaps best known for foursomes that move at approximately the same speed as continental drift. Without any marshals at public courses, play cannot be moved along at any sort of timed pace, so you'll see a lot of 30-yard tee shots, long consultations about club selections and rules about moving the ball, and fifteen minute putting sessions that include conversations about recipes.

$20,001 to $200,000 per year: Most people in this range tend to play at golf courses that are privately owned but open to the public. This would probably be the demographic bulk of the typical golfing public, the top of the bell curve of plaid Sansabelts and goofy golf hats. Let us note some of the typical characteristics of these courses:

1. A well-stocked, pleasingly tacky bar with cardiovascularly incorrect cuisine. Municipal public courses don't emphasize the booze part of their services, so it is up to the private sector to fill in the breach/glass/bottle. Like many sports that can be performed without dangerously elevating the heart rate to aerobic conditioning levels, golf can be and usually is performed under the influence of alcohol. Scientific studies have shown that golfing while tanked is an effective counterbalance to the otherwise stressful pursuit of par scores. In addition, the life-giving bar/snack shop food available at the privately owned public course provides essential "golf nutrients," such as animal fat for body bulking, sugar for quick energy, and salt for crucial water retention.

2. Fascinating pro shop banter. A regular McLaughlin Group of golf wisdom and aphorisms can be yours if you'll just open your ears at the glass counter of the pro shop. This free advice, handed down from generation to generation of mediocre golfers, does not end at the subject of the links, either. You can hear underemployed people insightfully criticize the president of the United States and the U.S. Congress for their lazy habits and get up-to-the-minute updates about what particular bit of witty by-play was on Rush Limbaugh that morning.

Above $200,001 per year: This is Valhallaville. You're playing on a course that was designed by Robert Trent Jones on his very best day, private to the extent that people whose families haven't been in this country 350 years

are put on a special waiting list. The water hazards are filled daily with fresh Evian, the sand traps are made from diamond chips, and the grass has been specially bred to never grow. Valet service on the golf carts. Caddies who have Ph.Ds in English Literature. Marshals dressed in black tie. Cocktail carts on every other tee. You're getting the picture.

Sometimes, if you're living in a far-flung Western state where riffraff are tolerated, you can buy your way into a club like this. It may only set you back $50 grand, not including green fees.

The best way to get into a situation like this is to be a member of a family that made the decision to buy a membership in 1935. Then they'll only give you a saliva test for admittance.

Disadvantages: If you don't shoot in the seventies with clockwork regularity, you'll be asked to leave and come back in 20 years with serious legal documentation that your game has improved. Another disadvantage is that you'll have to get used to drinking martinis.

Live with it.

How to Select a Putter

Of all the mysticism about golf, no one item is more shrouded in quasi-religious metaphysical yammering than the putter. Psychologists would probably give you a pretty straightforward Freudian explanation for a long hard object that causes something to go into a hole, but that's another book. What is it about putter selection that places it above, say, the six iron?

Well, first, the six iron is the most boring club in the bag. No one uses it. You hear a lot of discussion about the nine iron, for example, and rightly so. But no one agonizes over the six iron. You hit a soft five or whack the shit out of seven. The six is the cleanest iron in the bag. You might as well leave the plastic on.

The putter, however, is the most discussed club in your arsenal. Prayers are said to the putter. The putter is invoked in obscure Catholic liturgy. Votive candles are lit when people are about to putt. Abandon all hope, ye who putter here. And so on. The reason that the putter is so widely held forth upon is that it's the only club that's designed to actually put the ball in the hole—the object of the game. It's the putter, stupid.

Which putter is right for you? I like any putter that costs over 75 bucks. It's a good rule of thumb: just like paying, say, at least $75 grand for a car is a good rule of thumb. All other criteria are bunkum.

Oh, sure, you've got your little dots and lines and crosses on certain putters, but let's face it: God puts that ball in the hole, not the putter. What you really need is a dependable Western religion or Eastern philosophical tradition to fall back on when you putt—not some expensive piece of metal that will just let you down.

Golf as Religion

Golf is entering the realm of sports that have clearly evolved from mere games into Higher Pursuits. It happened to fly fishing a couple of years ago, and now it's happening to golf. Let us explore the theological possibilities pro and con of golf.

THE CASE FOR GOLF AS A RELIGION

1. You hear God's and Jesus's names a lot on the course, particularly around greens.
2. Golf has its holy icons, like Arnold Palmer and that John 3:16 guy.
3. Making a shot over a water hazard or out of a sand trap can be hell.
4. Golf is a quiet, contemplative pursuit, mostly after you're done playing.
5. It is just as expensive to buy golf accessories as to tithe ten percent to a church.
6. Golfers start worshipping inanimate objects, like their drivers.
7. Non-believers who don't share your fervor may think you're nuts.
8. Rituals and incantations are performed, and conversions experienced, when certain shots are made.
9. The surroundings are heavenly.
10. God is proven to exist when you make a ninety-foot putt.

Irresponsible Golf Tips for Beginners

Oftentimes you, as a responsible member of the golfing establishment, will have to golf with a beginner. Specifically, a beginner you do not care for. The temptation to give such a person really misleading golf tips is almost overpowering, and you must, from time to time, give in to that malevolent urge, if only to keep the golfing population down. It's a kind of golf Darwinism, a Malthusian paradigm of the links. Hence, these strictly misanthropic wrongheaded golf tips:

- Pull your head up before you hit the ball, to ensure that you will be able to see the ball as it travels down the fairway.
- When putting, use your wrists to do all the work—to provide proper "torque" to place the ball in the hole.
- Keep your body standing at attention at all times when swinging, to make sure the arms have a proper "stationary base."
- Buff all your club heads with hand soap. Let it dry on the club face, assuring a proper "safety cushion" between the club and the ball.
- Angrily challenge your partner's golf score at every hole, and accuse him of shaving two strokes per hole. (Actually, you could be telling the truth here.)
- Encourage the nascent golfer to use the new long-distance "whiffle" golf balls. Explain convincingly that the holes contribute less drag than a solid ball. TRY NOT TO LAUGH.
- Tell the new golfer about the hot new "electric club head snugs" for drivers, to keep the metal or wood pliable.
- Mention that he or she should hold the wedge backwards in the bunker, to "drive" the ball out of the sand.

What to Say to the Person Who Always Asks You, "What Club Are You Using?"

What do you say to the person whose conversational skills are limited to a short continuous tape loop which plays the message, "What club are you using?" Why do they ask this? They're out there on the course with, presumably, their own clubs, but on every swing they bleat the question about club selection. Well, other than asking them to please direct the question to your attorney, you can always give them the standard reply that I give anyone who asks me what club I'm using, which is: "Five iron."

Here's why it's the perfect response:

1. It sounds authoritative.
2. The five iron may well be the proper club in certain situations.
3. It shuts them up.
4. If it isn't the right club, they're obviously not going to know it.
5. It's better than telling them to please shut the hell up.
6. If it's not the right club, well, it's not like it's against the rules to tell them the wrong club.
7. Nothing the matter with a five iron, really.
8. Many tournament pros use a five iron.
9. Could work . . .
10. Hey, it's not an exact science.

User-Friendly Golf Holes

1. "THE FUNNEL HOLE." 5th Hole, Par One, 312 yards, Enigma Country Club, West Islip, Long Island, New York.

The 5th hole at Enigma features a long, downward sloping fairway of tightly cut grass which tapers into a virtually nonskid vortex at the green. According to all known laws of physics, a hole in one is guaranteed, unless your drive goes backwards off the tee.

2. "THE RELIGION HOLE." 16th Hole, Par Three, 345 yards, Our Mother of Holy Redemption Country Club, Vatican City.

The 16th hole at Our Mother of Holy Redemption features an inexplicable hole where all possible approach shots make it onto the green, usually within a few feet of the pin. A golfer could be situated behind an oak tree with a trunk six feet in diameter, in elephant grass, 260 yards from the green, on the next fairway over and, well, *something happens*. Shots get made. Enough said.

3. "THE LILLI-PUTT HOLE." 8th Hole, Par Five, 26 yards, Elmo's Pitch-'N'-Putt, Hot Springs, Arkansas.

This is the shortest PGA-sanctioned par five hole in the United States. Originally constructed as an elaborate practical joke, the 8th green at Elmo's is reachable with a real soft sand wedge. Once you're on the green, a staff member of the golf course will then move your ball within six inches of the hole when you're not looking. There is no additional charge for this service.

4. "THE GIMME HOLE." 12th Hole, Par Four, 416 yards, Commonweal Municipal Golf Course, Omaha, Nebraska.

From the tee, the Gimme Hole appears to be a garden variety par four. Use the Big Hammer to drive, maybe a five iron for your approach, chip on. Once you're on the green, however, things get a little easier. On the very large green are 75 individual holes, making that putt a bit easier. Every putt is a gimme here. A real scoresaver.

Teed-Off

If you want to know how the engine of capitalism runs, you should talk to the person who invented the golf tee. Minimum materials and technology, maximum profit. How much money is a tee worth? How many tees to make one fireplace log? How much is a cord of wood?

Well, let's say there could be 2,000 tees in a space the size of an average fireplace log. Maybe 300 logs in a cord of wood. That's 600,000 tees in a cord. A cord is about $100 now, give or take. Or, at 33 cents per log, a tee works out to .000165 cents. Now, let's express that in terms the average golfer can understand: A golfer, at pro shop prices, will pay $1 for 25 tees, or four cents per tee.

That's even better than defense contractors do on toilet seats.

Let us explore the function of the tee. First, why do we only get to use a tee when we tee off? A tee in the bunker would be helpful, wouldn't it? But no. Some rule fascist made some decision in 1356—now we're all paying the price.

There are also the new biodegradable tees. Not to be too much of a weenie environmentalist or anything, but it seems to me that when you consider that a golf course is a nightmare of wasteful fertilizers and clear-cut trees (not that I care, mind you—my dad used to work for the Forest Service), it seems a little silly to worry about whether your tees are biodegradable. Oh, well.

The tee, unlike most everything else in golf, cannot really be made fancier than its function demands. A tee made of a precious metal would probably bend and sure as hell isn't biodegradable. But the tee occupies a disproportionate amount of golf lexicon for its size: Tee time, tee off, practice tee, etc. All about a little piece of wood that costs 24,000 times less than you paid for it.

That can tee a person off.

CORD OF WOOD:
$100.00

CORD OF TEES:
$24,000.00

The Generic Pros

No matter what the decade, it seems there are always a certain number of pros on the tour who fit a certain profile. It doesn't matter what their names are, and for legal purposes as well as the desire to avoid having a three wood wrapped around my throat, these pros will remain nameless. But these guys are always on the tube, making the big shots and hauling down seven figures for putting their signatures on golf paraphernalia. It could be that these personality types are attracted to golf, just as people who look like Elvis tend to gravitate to stock racing. Let's examine the generic pros.

THE WINDSWEPT BLOND SQUINTY PRO

WHERE THEY COME FROM: A special breeding camp in Ohio where a stud team of low melanin, low handicap golfers meets regularly to flood the PGA Tour with these toothy guys with bottle-blonde hair and no discernable eyeballs.

USUAL NAMES: Johnny, Johnnie, Jon, John, Jack.

ENDORSEMENT POTENTIAL: Astronomical. Squinty blond guys average $3.8 million per year on endorsement contracts. Just on hair products alone.

PERSONAL LIVES: Disgustingly clean-cut, five little blond kids and a wife who actually looks good in golf dresses. Religious in a nonthreatening, Norman Rockwellian sort of way. Say things like, "Darn the luck" and "Shoot" and "Dang it all anyway," instead of standard Anglo-Saxon epithets.

GOLF GAME: Plodding but effective. Seem to have incorporated every good golf habit ever taught in their swing. Never get rattled, never blow a putt, never hit a bunker. Like watching a golf cyborg.

GOLF TIP: "Keep your head down and your eye on the Lord."

INEXPLICABLY ANGRY YOUNG BAD BOY PRO

Although they seemingly have the world on a tee, the Tour always seems to have some 26-year-old guy who has Richard Pryor, Jerry Lee Lewis, and Mike Tyson as his personal behavioral role models. The Angry Young Bad Boy is generally entertaining for golf writers, who have to, of necessity, write more about the mechanics of the game, rather than fisticuffs at the 15th hole.

WHERE THEY COME FROM: Small southern states that may still be in the Confederacy without our knowledge.

USUAL NAMES: Bud, Buddy, Bobby Joe, Bobby Ray, Bobby Anything.

ENDORSEMENT POTENTIAL: Wildly fluctuating between convictions.

PERSONAL LIVES: Married to women 20 years older than they are, no kids that they've been legally informed about. Lots of traffic citations, possibly minor criminal convictions such as throwing furniture out of 22nd floor hotel room windows, driving on railroad tracks, unregistered large caliber firearms possessions, contributing to the delinquency of girls who "didn't look a day under 14," and public urination at awards banquets.

GOLF GAME: Tend to be the most talented golfers on the tour. Aggressive style of play, including making armpit noises when other golfers tee off.

GOLF TIP: "Kids, golf, and cocaine just don't mix."

CHUBBY REGULAR GUY PRO

It can be reliably demonstrated that there are only two sports in the world where aerobic unfitness is no barrier to great success: stock car racing and golf. Hence, you will see many guys on the tour who probably couldn't do a mile in under fifteen minutes, and that's in a golf cart. This reassuring presence of regular guyness on the Tour is possibly what has contributed to the massive and growing popularity of golf itself: the notion that it is physically democratic.

WHERE THEY COME FROM: Regular places like Indiana, Illinois, and Michigan.

USUAL NAMES: Chuck, Tom, Ed, Greg, Craig, Bob.

ENDORSEMENT POTENTIAL: Limited, but potentially lucrative. You can pretty well bag the underwear ads, but you're looking at Ultra Slim-Fast, lawnmower, and Sansabelt contracts without end.

PERSONAL LIVES: Nondescript. Wife, two kids, usual drill. Hobbies include domestic beer tasting and White Owl cigars.

GOLF GAME: Often spectacular, particularly considering the outward appearance of the player.

GOLF TIP: "This goddamn Master's Jacket doesn't fit anymore, honey!"

Golf Channel Listings

With the establishment of a cable channel devoted strictly to golf—heck, why not? there's a Luftwaffe Channel—there comes the problem of how to structure the program day. They can't just run tournaments all the time, so they'll undoubtably have to have other programming. Let's look at a proposed broadcast day.

5:00 AM: "Let's Tee Off!" Wake-up golf music.

5:30 AM: "Golf Spike Week in Review."

6:00 AM: "The Lord Is My Caddy." Inspirational.

6:30 AM: "The General Dynamics/Rockwell International/Raytheon Invitational." Live from the Pentagon Golf Course.

8:00 AM: "The Divotheads." Golf family sitcom starring Dick Van Patten, and the Van Patten children, all of whom look like golfers.

8:30 AM: "Don't Cut That Golf Ball!" A whimsical look at those wacky people who tried to find the acid in the center. From the Houston Memorial Hospital Burn Unit.

9:00 AM: "Teach Your Pet to Golf." This episode: Spuds McKenzie on putting.

9:30 AM: "The Swingers." Sex instruction video.

10:00 AM: "Those Deadly Golfers." A look at Jerry Ford and Spiro Agnew.

10:30 AM: "The Tide Detergent Cambodia Open." Tournament highlights.

11:00 AM: "Golf Crossfire" On the right: Arnold Palmer. On the left: Tom Kite. Guests: John Deeremulching Mower, Executive Director of People for the Ethical Treatment of Kentucky Bluegrass, and Sandy Bunker, President, "Golf First!"

11:30 AM: "The Maalox Pennzoil Shearson Lehman STP Skins Game." Live from Dogma Heights Country Club in Gatorsville, Florida.

NOON: "Eyewitness GolfCenter NewsScan."

12:30 PM: "Pebble Beach 90210" A group of overly attractive teens hang out at the golf course, agonizing over their adolescence and their golf swings.

1:00 PM: "Golf Weather Update."

1:30 PM: "Political Hackers." Taped highlights of our nation's congressmen as they play as the guests of lobbyists from huge multinational corporations. (Closed captioned for the ethics impaired.)

2:00 PM: "World O' Six Irons."

2:30 PM: "The 19th Hole Sponsored by Budweiser." Golf's greatest drunks get together and lie about their game.

3:00 PM: "The Clearasil Invitational." Live from the Hormonal Peak Country Club in Taos, New Mexico. The hottest teen golfers in America compete for the keys to Jack Nicklaus's car.

4:30 PM: "Speaking of Golf Injuries." With Doc Legright. Today: Why your rotator cuff has to obey the laws of physics.

5:00 PM: "Alan Shepard's Most Difficult Shots In Golf." This episode: Venus.

5:30 PM: "The Mitsubishi Honda Sanyo Sony Toyota Open." Live from Detroit, Michigan. Japan's greatest golfers rub it in.

6:00 PM: "Give Me That Goddamn Driver, I'll Show You." How to teach your spouse to golf.

6:30 PM: "The Masters of Miniature Golf."

7:00 PM: "The 150 Club." The nation's poorest golfers compete for the right to quit golfing entirely.

7:30 PM: "Spotlight on Club Covers."

8:00 PM: "Winter Rules." How to improve your cheating.

8:30 PM: "Those Golfing Presidents." Computer simulation of a competing foursome of Dwight Eisenhower, Millard Fillmore, John Quincy Adams, and George Bush.

9:00 PM: "The St. Andrews Show." Scottish golf call-in.

9:30 PM: "Assault Golf." How a semiautomatic weapon in your bag can speed up the foursome ahead of you.

10:00 PM: "My Three Putts." A man gets the yips after playing with his three dopey sons.

10:30 PM: "The Depend Undergarment Geritol Centrum Silver Classic." Taped highlights of annual tournament played by "Today Show" centenarians.

11:00 PM: "Marshal Law." Action adventure. When play slows down, the country club golf marshals take the law and .44 magnums into their own hands.

11:30 PM: "Top-Flite Presents the Biggest Balls in Golf."

MIDNIGHT: Movie *How Green Was My Green*, BW, 1943. Greer Garson, Bing Crosby, Peter Lorre.

3:00 AM: Movie *Murder at the Driving Range*, Color, 1986. Loni Anderson, John Ritter.

The Hole Golf Catalog

THE BLOND GOLF PRO WIG

Have you noticed that more than 70 percent of all the golfers in the world have long, limp blond hair with an almost iridescent sheen? Now you can achieve that "golf pro" look, even if you're bald! The Blond Golf Pro Wig is that tonsorial statement you need to cut 15 strokes from your game. The Golf Pro Wig has been used by tens of thousands of satisfied golfers and has accounted for over $90 million in pretax PGA-sanctioned tournament winnings. The Golf Pro Wig just glues or velcros right onto your scalp or existing wrong color hair; there are no messy straps or telltale adjustable springs. The Golf Pro Wig comes in its own fashionable high-impact polystyrene case and slips easily into your golf bag. Color: blond only. Price: $349.95

THE HEAD DOWN INSTRUCTIONAL BRACE

Tired of always pulling your head up at the last possible second and fluffing your shot? The Head Down Instruction Brace is the answer. The Head Down Instructional Brace fits easily over your entire body. The lightweight yet durable "Golf-Lite" structural steel and semicollapsible aluminum frame takes only hours to snap and weld into place. An ingenious "Help-N-Halo" bolts directly into your skull to keep your head immobile during all phases of the swing. A solid molybedenum and lead "Foot Locker" keeps those feet standing in the proper position. Breaks down into a fairly manageable 400-pound carrying case. Not for use by children or sadomasochists. Colors: Silver, camouflage. Price: $4,850.00

The
HEAD
DOWN
INSTRUCTIONAL
BRACE

THE DOGGY CADDY

Lugging your own clubs around can be a real burden. The strap digs into your shoulder, causing vital golf muscles to tire and eventually collapse in key golf situations, embarrassing you and possibly costing you a buck a hole. The solution is ARFCO's Doggy Caddy. The Doggy Caddy is simple: Bring Fido along for companionship and as a beast of burden. Just strap your lovable mutt into the easy adjusting golf bag frame, and you're ready to play. Doggy does the work, which frees you up to slaughter your opponents on the links while your canine pal humps your clubs around. Plus, the Doggy Caddy doesn't give you any of that patronizing golf advice that you usually get with a 14-year-old boy. Please specify dog size when ordering. Not recommended for dogs under 40 pounds. $785.99

GOLF KART KUSTOM KIT

The trouble with golf carts is that they all look the same. But with the new Golf Kart Kustom Kit, you can tear up the links in a way you never thought possible. A golf cart with headers? No problem! A roll bar and rear balloon tires? Just say the words. A flame insignia and dual exhaust pipes? Just slap 'em on. Need to go "off road" into some really heavy rough? Four wheel drive, a light bar, and a winch might help. The Golf Kart Kustom Kit komes komplete—excuse us—comes complete with detailed instructions, a ball peen hammer, a can of Bondo, and an instructional video on putting. Price: $22,500.00

FOURSOME WARNING RIFLE

No doubt there's been more than one time when you've really wanted to speed up play up on the next green. It seems like the dodos ahead of you are personally inspecting every blade of grass on the green, checking the fringe for weed invasions, and regaling each other with boring childhood reminiscences. What to do? Send 'em a warning—shot, that is. Try the new Foursome Warning Rifle from Pyng Arms. Easily concealed in any regulation-size golf bag (check local gun laws), the Foursome Warning Rifle packs a real wallop: a 30.06 slug traveling at 3,000 feet per second, which makes an ear-shattering "Crack-BARRR-ROOOOOOOOOOOOM!!!!!!" audible for miles around. One warning shot over their heads should be plenty, but if they persist, well, they asked for it. Colors: Tan, Forest Green, Camouflage. Price: $399.95

THE ROUGH MORTAR

How many times have you found yourself in heavy, Vietnam-canopy-type rough, completely invisible to your playing partners, unable to make any sort of shot due to the incredibly dense undergrowth? For some of us, it's a way of life; hacking our way through the brush, trying to make the impossible shot through thick trees, swearing and sweating all the way. Well, those days are over at last, thanks to the Rough Mortar. The Rough Mortar is simple: just drop in any make of golf ball, adjust the altitude and azimuth, count three and listen for the distinctive "THUNK!" Presto! You're on the green! And with a totally legal, if incendiary, club. Price: $3,599.99

SCORECARD ALTERATION KIT

Let's face it, nobody likes to get caught cheating on their score. But, as every true golfer knows, sometimes cheating is the difference between winning and losing, between humiliating your boss or being humiliated by him. Beat the system with the Scorecard Alteration Kit. There's a reason why those golf course scoring pencils don't have an eraser: to prevent against unsightly or detectable score fudging. But with the Scorecard Alteration Kit, you can neatly and convincingly airbrush not only your score but par numbers on the holes, opponents' scores— "Gee, no, Brad, I'm sorry, you got a seven on the thirteenth hole, not a five. Don't you remember?"—and many other applications we haven't thought of yet. Takes ten strokes off your game instantly. Makes a great gift for the felonious hacker. Price: $23.95

THE HAZARD DRAIN

Making that long shot over the water hazard isn't fun: It's stressful. And golf is supposed to be fun, right? An escape from stress, correct? And water hazards eat up a lot of balls every year. Get rid of them for good with the Hazard Drain. The Hazard Drain is simple to use. It requires no knowledge of hydrology to operate, and it works like a dream. Just screw the Hazard Drain into any water hazard, flowing or not, and watch your troubles and tensions ease as the water flows into any nearby aquifer. And don't forget to pick up the 1,679 balls you'll find at the bottom! Price: $129.99

BUNKER GRASS PATCH

What could be a bigger pain in the butt than attempting to chip out of a bunker? You've got to line that wedge up just right behind the ball, blast it out, and then rake up all that messy sand. But with the revolutionary Bunker Grass Patch, those days are gone for good. When your fellow golfers aren't looking, stealthily drop the Bunker Grass Patch into the sand. Put your ball on it and swing as you normally would. If you're not a complete spaz, you're off the beach and into the nice cool green grass. The Bunker Grass Patch comes in its extremely subtle carrying case, too! It's disguised as a box of Titleists and slips in and out of your golf bag like a burglar. Don't get "trapped" again! Color: Green only. Price $39.95

THE BUNKER GRASS PATCH

THE VIRTUAL REALITY GOLF SUIT

Sometimes it's just not possible to golf. It's raining or snowing, or you don't have all afternoon to play. With the Virtual Reality Golf Suit, you make the call when you want to play. Developed by the Japanese, who pay $2,000 green fees, the Virtual Reality Golf Suit slips on easily over any clothing, and is equipped with over 240 tiny micro sensors to provide high-touch, high-tech golf fun. Just grab the Micro-Chipper Club Interface System, and swing away. Requires only 60 cubic feet to play, and there are no green fees. Enjoy a virtual drink at the virtual 19th hole after your game. Price: 980,000,000 yen.

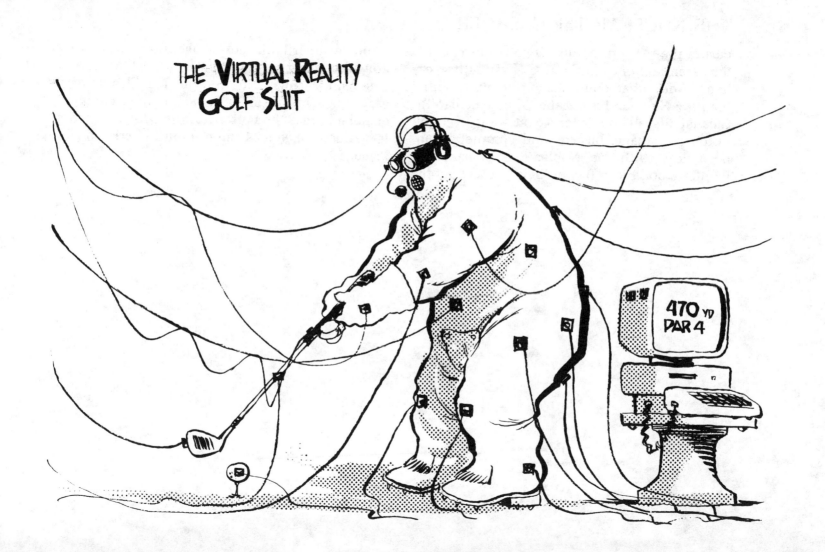

THE NUCLEAR TEE CLEANER

Part of the real fun of buying golf equipment is the essential nonessentialness of virtually every item. And what could be more nonessential than the Nuclear Tee Cleaner? The Nuclear Tee Cleaner fits all the criteria you want in a golf purchase: arcane, bizarre, and completely unnecessary. With the Nuclear Tee Cleaner by PaintedWood Fiber Technologies, you've got the ultimate superfluous golf gadget that will drive nongolfers crazy. And after all, isn't that what you really want? The Nuclear Tee Cleaner is easy to use: Just insert your tee into the cleaning chamber, press the button, and presto! Your tee is perfectly clean 24 short hours later! Wow! Price: $675.99

THE NUCLEAR
TEE CLEANER

ON

WHITE TEE

COLORED
TEE

THE INCREDIBLY LONG, BORING, BADLY PRODUCED GOLF INSTRUCTIONAL VIDEO FEATURING NO ONE YOU'VE EVER HEARD OF

All golfers want to improve their games, so they often resort to instructional videos. Well, Blurry Video has produced the longest, dullest golf video of all time. It's more complicated than a Kurosawa movie, has all the production values of a stag film, and is hosted by some assistant pro at a par three pitch-and-putt golf course in Indiana. How's that for obscure? But there's more. You'll never learn a thing from this video because we've recorded the audio track in Russian! We'll cover the fundamentals of golf, all right, and in the most excruciating manner possible, because this video is over 13 hours in length. You can watch this tape for hours and never get a thing out of it. And after all, is it really any different from any other golf video? Shot in grainy black and white with lots of interference. Price: $69.95

The Unpublished Missing Rules of Golf

Like the Dead Sea Scrolls, there has long been dispute about the authenticity of the so-called "Missing Rules" of golf. Golf scholars, of whom there are more than you might think, given all the things to worry about in the world, have argued endlessly over the "Missing Rules" until punches were thrown or clubs were jammed into orifices. Here then are the "Missing Rules," and judge for yourself their authenticity. Found in a bunker near "The Road Hole" at the Old Course at St. Andrews in 1967, the rules were taken to the USGA headquarters and carbon dated. They were then placed in a safe deposit box in Columbus, Ohio. They are reprinted here for the first time.

RULE 35-1. Swearing at Your Partner During Play. A player may not invoke any Anglo-Saxon rejoinders, descriptions of "normal" bodily functions, Judeo-Christian–based invective, or references to ancestry which is directed at a fellow player. It is legal to direct it at the ball.

RULE 35-2. Throwing of Clubs During Play. Players may throw more than the prescribed 14 clubs (not including bag) only if a fellow player's clubs are included and the throwing player is properly billed. The clubs must be thrown in an undirected manner. Targeted throwing of clubs at a fixed object, such as a fellow golfer, is not legal, unless the targeted golfer has made a mutually agreed upon Derogatory Remark.

RULE 35-3. Derogatory Remark During Play. A golfer may not make a Derogatory Remark, unless it is clearly under the breath. "Under the breath" is described in USGA Rules of Golf as a "remark quieter than 20 dB and not employing aforementioned uncouth language, but merely commenting on the competency of the fellow golfer."

RULE 35-4. Snorting or Distracting Animal Noises During Tee Offs or Putting. No barnyard noises shall be made by an opposing golfer or interested member of the gallery. Barnyard

noises may be made during approach shots providing the noise-making golfer is one hundred (100) yards in distance from the other golfers.

Barnyard noises shall be defined as "snorting, grunting, howling, yipping, barking, hooting, or making rooting noises," according to USGA Rules of Golf.

RULE 35-5. Out of Bounds Definitions by Condo or Home Owners Lining a Fairway in a Golf Course Development. Homeowners building a house or condominium directly interfacing or contiguous to a USGA-sanctioned golf course may not define out of bounds except when a personal possession valued at more than $5,000 is deemed at risk by a golf swing. Geranium beds, fake flamingoes, bizarre statuary, rose bushes, mulch, compost heaps, peony gardens, tulip bulbs are all adjudicated to be within acceptable boundaries and are legal surfaces upon which a golfer may hit a regulation golf ball.

RULE 36-1. Water Hazard Wading. A golfer may not wade more than 50 feet from riparian boundaries established by the meniscus of the water adjoining the physically established edge or shoreline of a water hazard, unless all golfing clothes are removed in full view of any passing foursomes, so that the physique of the golfer may be commented upon for flaws. Clothes may be stolen or "confiscated" by any other observing player for the remainder of the golfer's round but must be returned to the golfer at the clubhouse. A drowning golfer must be submerged for two (2) minutes in order to be considered "drowning" in a clinical sense and thus subject to outside medical intervention. A player who drowns while attempting to retrieve a ball will be assessed a 2-stroke penalty.

RULE 36-2. Open Weeping. Open weeping is a USGA-approved legally sanctioned method of expressing an emotion after the poor or incompetent execution of a particularly critical golf shot. A one-stroke penalty may be assessed if the weeping is conducted within ten feet of a golfer who is making a shot.

RULE 36-3. Wailing, Gnashing of Teeth. Wailing and gnashing teeth are illegal expressions of emotion and will be assessed a two-stroke penalty.

RULE 36-4. Inappropriate Golf Headgear. Inappropriate golf headgear is defined as any:

a. Plastic or petroleum-based adjustable baseball caps with a foam rubber front advertising products not normally associated with the game of golf, such as fishing tackle, alcoholic beverages made from hops and grain, and automotive supplies or services.

b. Baseball-style caps of any material composition that have integrated into their design large, distracting additions such as horns, antennae, propellers, antlers, arrows, or any other addenda deemed inappropriate by the USGA.

c. Straw- or grass-based hat with a brim wider than three feet that is colored other than a range from white to tan.

d. Other hats that call into question the mental stability of the wearer or distract other golfers from their normal styles of play, including helmets, military-style officers caps, Carmen Miranda fruit headpieces, or gangster-style fedoras.

Golf Law

While the Rules of Golf seems legalistic, shouldn't there be actual Golf Law, to cover any judicial/golfing situation? Couldn't there be golf lawyers to argue these cases and golf courts to interpret them? In 1993, a test golf court of appeals was established in the Southern District of Florida, for the express purpose of establishing golf legal precedent. Southern Florida was chosen for its number of golfers and the demographic mix. These are the results of some of the early test cases in golf:

U.S. v. ALLIGATOR. In *U.S.* v. *Alligator*, the court ruled that it is illegal for alligators to eat golfers, unless a three-judge panel independently determined that the golfer's attire was so unsightly as to provoke the alligator, which then held the alligator harmless from prosecution or damages.

SCHLUBMAN v. LYNX. In *Schlubman* v. *Lynx*, it was ruled that a golf club manufacturer cannot be held responsible for the poor execution of a shot during match play. Plaintiff attempted to show malice in the manufacturer's design of the clubs, but defendant argued that lack of practice and no lessons were the actual culprits.

JUDSON v. FORSTROM. In *Judson* v. *Forstrom*, the plaintiff alleged that his partner, the defendant, was playing so poorly that the plaintiff's own concentration was blown for the remainder of the round. Jury found for the defendant when defendant's counsel pointed out that the plaintiff was making armpit noises during key intervals in the round to distract the defendant.

LEINFELTER v. KELLY. In *Leinfelter* v. *Kelly*, plaintiff alleged that the defendant was secretly keeping a journal of all the defendant's poor shots to be made into an instructional golf book. Defendant was unable to successfully refute charges. Journal was produced with such entries as, "Leinfelter killed a goose with a seven iron," and "Leinfelter lost six balls on one 187-yard par three hole." A three-judge panel ruled against defendant and ordered proceeds from the sales of the book to be split equally between plaintiff and defendant.

Club Selection

Perhaps one of the main keys to successful golf—oxymoron of the decade—is developing the ability to make the proper club selection. Aside from pestering your partner for advice, which we will deal with later, you must begin to rely on your long dormant instincts as a hunter-gatherer instead of a golfing wuss. Let's look at the different clubs and their uses. Remember, you're only allowed 14 clubs, and not one of them can save you.

THE DRIVER. A big piece of nonaerodynamic metal or persimmon that you should rightly be afraid of. Using the driver is kind of like watching a 747 take off. It's amazing that it works at all because of its size; and like the 747, in the wrong hands, it can be dangerous. There are known psychiatric disorders centered around the fear of drivers, and they are treatable only with drugs. Okay, they're only treatable with beer in the clubhouse after your round.

THE THREE WOOD. A medium-sized piece of nonaerodynamic metal or persimmon that you should rightly be afraid of.

THE FIVE WOOD. An inexplicably small wood that is the result of bonsai technology. It's a good club to use after a 60-foot tee shot.

THE THREE IRON. A good club to use after a 100-foot tee shot.

THE FOUR IRON. Throw it away. The cleanest club in the bag. Has never actually been used in PGA play.

THE FIVE IRON. Probably the most used club, it has the reputation of being a consensus club for shots that are of indeterminate distance: "Oh, what the hell . . . use the five iron, Bob."

THE SIX IRON. Second cleanest club in the bag. No one talks about it. Has no profile. The Ghost Club.

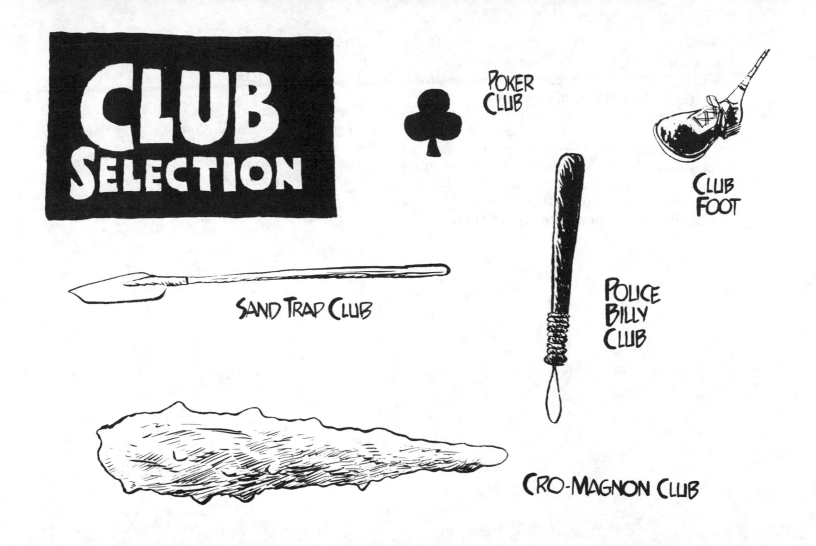

CLUB SELECTION

POKER CLUB

CLUB FOOT

SAND TRAP CLUB

POLICE BILLY CLUB

CRO-MAGNON CLUB

THE SEVEN IRON. A club that, by far, is one that you will always overshoot your target with, without exception, absolutely and positively guaranteed. Could be manufactured by the golf equipment industry as some sort of elaborate practical joke.

THE EIGHT IRON. Hardly ever used, again, because no one really is able to judge the difference between an eight-iron shot and a nine-iron shot. Everyone who's golfed more than a nano-second can recognize a nine-iron shot.

THE NINE IRON. The club you use to put the ball in the sand trap.

THE PITCHING WEDGE. The club you use to recover your nine iron shot out of the sand trap.

THE SAND WEDGE. The club you use to get your pitching wedge shot out of the far side of the sand trap.

THE PUTTER. Overly discussed, but let's give it its own chapter anyway (see page 16).

The Grip

The grip, like the swing, is one of those nasty little fundamentals that your golf instructor is always bellowing about. The first thing that could improve your grip is in the glove. Wrapping electrical tape around the fingers is an excellent way to maintain your grip through the crucial "holding onto" phase of the swing, which, if ignored, will result in the release of your club into the air and about 150 feet downrange from where your feet should be properly positioned.

Hint: Carry an extra bottle of Elmer's Glue-All for when the sweat from your hands caused by exceptionally bad play loosens your grip.

There are two types of grips. The most widely used grip is the "Improper Grip," which is utilized by about 85 percent of all golfers. This is the grip which will build up crucial open sores and callouses to cushion your club in the "ball address" portion of the swing.

The second most widely used grip is the "Interlocking Cross-Entwined Latticed Lock Grip," which is the choice of most PGA professionals (the office support staff, not the actual golfers). This is the grip that people who have three hours a day to practice use.

The grip is important not only in the "swinging" phase of your game. Come to think of it, swinging is the only phase of the game. Well, that and proper nonembarrassing clothing selection, which seems to be the toughest phase for most of the people you see on the links. The grip is also important in the temper tantrum portion of your game. A good grip means good distance when flinging your club into the nearest rough or water hazard.

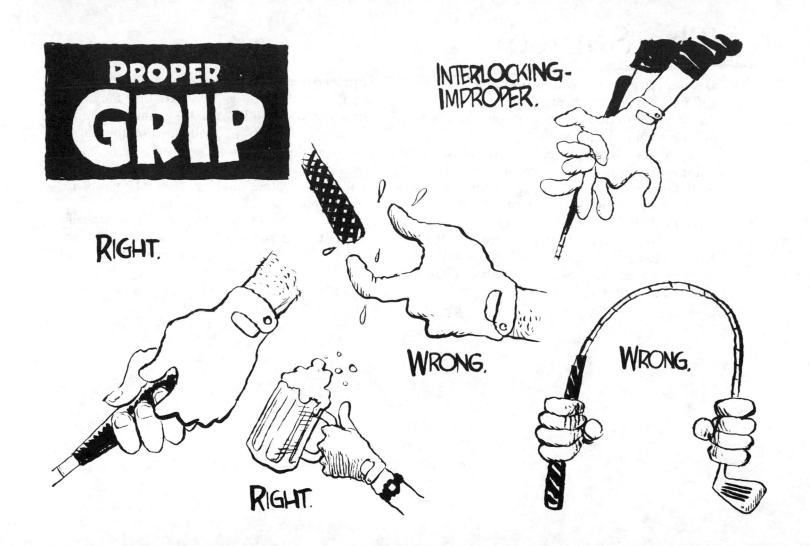

The Stance

Developing a proper stance is arguably the most difficult part of the game. Since most of us are couch potato Americans, we don't have a very good stance to begin with.

Try to visualize yourself as a tripod when developing a proper golf stance. Your legs are your, well, legs, and the club is your penis. Okay, let's not get too Freudian, particularly if you're a woman. The club is just your club.

First, stand somewhere near the ball. It's best to have the ball just slightly further away than you need it to be—that's the kind of challenge that makes golf exciting.

Second, look at your feet. Do they have USGA-approved expensive golf shoes on? Are they about the same relative size? Are they laughably large for your body? Do they have unsightly corns or bunions? Is your second toe longer than your big toe? If so, you may be a . . . oh, never mind. Anyway, it's best to consult a foot health care professional before entering into any golf regimen.

Third, put your right foot in. Put your right foot out. You put your right foot in and you shake it all about. You do the hokey pokey and you turn yourself around.

That's what it's all about.

What's in the Average Golf Bag?

Most people have golf bags that make serious statements about their intentions—if not their abilities—as golfers. For example, a skinny little plaid bag says, in short, "My mom bought this for me at a garage sale, and I know next to nothing about the game of golf." A monster bag says, "I'm a pretentious golfing dork who has absolutely no other interests in life and I'm quite possibly a doctor."

But what makes the greatest statement about you, as A Proud Golfing American, is the contents of your bag. A scientifically random sampling conducted by the Gallup organization (not affiliated with the real Gallup Organization) indicates that the contents of our bags may reflect the content of our psyches.

Here's what they found in the average bag:

- 13 clubs. (You left the wedge at home while practicing in the yard, and your dog is now having it for lunch.)
- 44 balls: two new Titleists, 13 "club special" cheapos out of the fishbowl at the pro shop counter, 16 cut balls, ten balls with various obscure corporate logos (mostly insurance or banking industry), three balls with someone else's name on them.
- No tees. (You're always "borrowing" them or picking the broken tee nubs out of the grass, like used cigar butts.)
- 16 wadded up golf ball boxes jammed into the smallest pocket.
- Someone else's rain jacket.
- Unidentifiable foodlike substance.
- One very warm domestic brand beer.
- One golf shoe covered with dried mud—the other shoe was left in the muck next to a water hazard.
- 89 scorecards from various courses, all virtually illegible because of constant rubbing in the bag.
- Two pencils that always poke you when you reach into bag.

Greatest Golf Movies of All Time

The golf movie, as a genre, hasn't exactly been given its cinematic due compared to, say, the baseball movie. Baseball movies, by and large, end in the untimely death of a major leaguer from some debilitating illness or bizarre accident. Or they wind up exploring the father-son relationship in such an unbelievably corny manner that grown men weep at the end out of embarrassment for the moviemaker, not at the memories of their fathers. Not so the golf movie. The golf movie, although little-watched and little-recognized, is an area movie historians have been increasingly turning their attention to, mostly out of boredom. The catalog of golf movies is a small but influential segment of the marketplace. Some of the best-loved golf movies include:

One Flew Over the Cuckoo's Nest and Landed Three Feet from the Pin. 1971. Jack Nicholson. Jack Nicklaus. A documentary examination of golf's greatest exaggerations, as narrated by Jack Nicholson and Jack Nicklaus.

Citizen Ping. 1938. Orson Welles. One of America's great golf magazine publishers goes insane and tries to get on the Tour.

How Green Was My Green. 1939. Greer Garson. The first woman golfer in Wales makes incredible putts and goes on to found the LPGA.

A Lateral Water Hazard Runs Through It. 1992. Tom Skerritt, Tom Kite, Tom Watson. A stoic Montana family can only communicate on the golf course.

On the Beach. 1959. Trevor Howard, Sir John Geilgud, Greg Norman. Australian golfers survive a nuclear war in a sand trap.

Field of Drivers. 1987. Kevin Costner, Bobby Jones. An Iowa farmer is instructed by a mysterious voice to build a championship 18-hole course on his farm.

Golf Slang

One of the really fun things about golf is all the neat slang terminology that you can employ to present yourself as real "hepcat" insider linkster. It's a lot easier than you think to memorize these key "golferisms" and liberally sprinkle them in everyday golf conversation, so as to amaze your friends with how tuned in you are to golf link lingo.

"Cutting the carpet and tacking it down": Too many divots.

"Bouncing off the Buicks": I guess a tee shot into the parking lot.

"Missed the subway": A bad putt.

"Having the grass salad with everything on it": Bad divot, maybe? I only heard it once in a bar.

"Reverse Pearl Harbor": Playing through a group of Japanese golf tourists.

"Racking up the frequent flier miles": Too many swings in a round.

"Teaching the dog to sing": Screaming at the top your lungs after a bad shot.

"Sacrifice to the graphite gods": Throwing your clubs in the water.

"Trying out the Big Ball Washer": Another Titleist into the drink.

"Follow the bouncing ball": Nice drive onto the cart path pavement.

"Looking for Atlantis": Attempting to fish your ball out of the water.

"Playing Neil and Buzz on the moon": Making nice footprints in the bunker.

"Swinging the big axe in Paul Bunyanville": Shooting from the woods.

"Filing an amended return": Lying about your golf score.

What Caddies Say

What You Say to the Caddy	What the Caddy Will Say	What the Caddy Is Thinking
"What club should I use?"	"Go with the five iron."	"Go with the five iron, obviously, dipshit."
"Can I clear that water?"	"Better give it a ride."	"Take a drop."
"Can I clear that tree?"	"Maybe with an eight."	"Maybe with an eight and an 80-mile-per-hour tailwind."
"How do you like my shirt?"	"Really cool, sir."	"Your mom still shops for you, and you're 52?"
"Well, I shot a four on the last hole."	"Yes, sir."	"Yeah, a four plus the three extra putts."
"Wash my balls."	"Yes, sir."	"What a straight line."
"Gee, that hole bends around the corner."	"This is true."	"We call it a dogleg in our language."
"That's a 79 for this round."	"Good round, sir."	"Might be a 79 in dog score."

The Least Popular Tournaments in the World

1. The Large Sweaty Guy Pro-Am
2. The Dan Quayle Intellectual Desert Classic
3. The Attacking Hyena Invitational
4. Dodge the Hanging Anaconda Zaire Classic
5. The Play Drunk With Large Caliber Weapons Open
6. The Forest Lawn Cemetery Scramble
7. The Eczema Skins Game
8. The Los Angeles Freeway Challenge
9. The K2 Sheer Rock Face Invitational
10. The Tournament of Condo Picture Windows Facing the Tee

MASTER'S JACKET.

SCHLUBVILLE C.C.
INVITATIONAL
JACKET.

Meet Your Golfing Partners

THE FRAT RAT

NAME: Charles Guernsey "Beef" Wellington III
AGE: 28
HOME: Atlanta, Georgia (Parents have resort homes in Aspen, Palm Springs, and Dataw Island.)
OCCUPATION: Securities Trainee, Merrill Lynch.
GOLF CURRICULUM VITAE: Heir to $11 million. Began golfing at three. Father made money in defense stocks. Had inside knowledge on Vietnam war, served six years for SEC violations, golfed at Allenwood Federal Minimum Security Prison, elected to Congress in 1974. Treasurer of fraternity at University of Virginia; expelled for cheating at golf, diverting frat money to Contras during Irangate. Golf team vice captain.
SPECIAL GOLF SKILLS: Hits six iron 270 yards holding Marlboro Light, brutally cold can of MeisterBrau, an airline bottle of Stoli, and his putter simultaneously.
HANDICAP: 2
GOLF HERO: Dan Quayle
GOLF QUOTE: "They say the 1980s were excessive, but they didn't see my golf scores."

THE LITTLE OLD LADY

NAME: Babe Blueharris
AGE: 70 something
HOME: Winter Haven, Florida
OCCUPATION: Retired, with 16 grandchildren. Would you like to see their pictures?
GOLF CURRICULUM VITAE: Started golfing last year.
SPECIAL GOLF SKILLS: Ambling at plate tectonic pace down center of fairway. Swinging in double digits at every hole. Losing ball in very short fairway grass. Talking about grandchildren to her foursome and others on the green. Nine-putting. Taking seven minutes to find her grip on tee-off. Helping others find teeth in rough.
HANDICAP: Golfs the year she was born, as opposed to her age.
GOLF HERO: Dinah Shore
GOLF QUOTE: "I can't find my ball. Can you find my ball? I don't see the ball."

THE TWICE-A-YEAR GOLFER

NAME: Rube Hacker
AGE: 56
HOME: Hackensack, New Jersey
OCCUPATION: A not terribly successful insurance guy.
GOLF CURRICULUM VITAE: Goes golfing twice a year, generally at the insistence of some well-meaning friend who says, "You need to get out and get some fresh air, relax, and golf." Owns own clubs (Montgomery Ward starter set from 1959, plaid bag, naturally). Needs to be resuscitated after every round. Gets very, very mad.

SPECIAL GOLF SKILLS: Screaming at top of lungs after blowing out rotator cuff while swinging. Misses ball every other swing. Has one good shot per round and brags about it. Getting hammered in clubhouse after cardiac-inducing round. Vows to quit golf after playing round.
HANDICAP: In the low four figures.
GOLF HERO: Had a golf pro in the family once and constantly reminds people of that fact.
GOLF QUOTE: "Why do I keep playing this god-damned game? My cardiologist says to give it up."

MR. BRAND NAME EQUIPMENT

NAME: Max Goldcard

AGE: 39

HOME: Lawnguyland, New York

OCCUPATION: Comptroller of an investment house featured in a major book about the rapaciousness of the 1980s.

GOLF CURRICULUM VITAE: Needed to start golfing for business reasons. Spends equivalent of Bolivian debt on equipment every year. Owns over 1,700 putters. Is referred to as "Your Royal Indebtedness" at the pro shop. Buys tee cleaners. Has every golf mug ever made. Collection of golf books is larger than the PGA headquarters.

SPECIAL GOLF SKILLS: Set course record for total season divot tonnage at home country club. Nicknamed "The Backhoe" by marshals. Has never broken 150.

HANDICAP: I said has never broken 150. You figure it out.

GOLF HERO: Anyone who has ever signed an endorsement deal with a golf-related corporation.

GOLF QUOTE: "I can get you a deal on those Pings, but I gotta make some calls."

ANCIENT GOLF HOLY MAN

NAME: Olden Wise

AGE: Who knows? Played with Bobby Jones. Actually, coached him.

HOME: Perhaps a mountaintop

OCCUPATION: Golf pro at an exclusive Southern private club since the Wilson administration.

GOLF CURRICULUM VITAE: Has tutored every pro on the Tour since the invention of grass. Is said to communicate in an ancient dead language that is not dissimilar to speaking in tongues. Golfers come away from a lesson glassy-eyed and stammering, then shave ten to 15 strokes off their games. Golfers who touch the hem of his garment usually shoot par golf for the rest of their life. Jack Nicklaus is known to begin wailing and sobbing uncontrollably at the mere mention of his name. Shafts of light cut down through the clouds when he walks on the course. Walks on water hazards.

SPECIAL GOLF SKILLS: Aren't those enough?

HANDICAP: Is a Perfect Golfer. Once shot an 18.

GOLF HERO: Speaks with a deceased Scottish golfer from the 1400s.

GOLF QUOTE: "Go, and pull your head up no more."

THE GOLF HUSTLER

NAME: Withheld pending outcome of grand jury investigation

AGE: 66

HOME: Various federal penal institutions when not out on parole

OCCUPATION: Golf Entrepreneur/Hustler

GOLF CURRICULUM VITAE: Wanders around clubhouse asking new-looking guys to show him how to hold his club and then offers to pay them for a lesson. Gets them on the course, offers to make a "friendly sportin'-type wager," gives them a stroke per hole, and the rest is history. Competes in World Series of Poker. Made the Tour in '64, shot a 66 at Pebble Beach, but left Tour in '78, after attempting to fix the Masters.

SPECIAL GOLF SKILLS: Is able to make "optical illusion" shots. Has devised a workable method of sending mind control messages to his partners. Insists on Match Play. Successfully counterweighted a golf ball without getting acid sprayed in his face. Won $1,666,000 in a game with a guy from Kuwait. Knows how to hot-wire golf carts.

HANDICAP: To you, it's 20. It's actually 3.

GOLF HERO: John Dillinger

GOLF QUOTE: "I'd like to speak to an attorney."

THE SURBURBAN LADY GOLFER

NAME: Mrs. Robinson
AGE: Not all that old, really
HOME: Greenwich, Connecticut
OCCUPATION: Homemaker
GOLF CURRICULUM VITAE: Golfs every day. Has a handicap 12 strokes lower than her husband's. Has pictures of Nancy Lopez all over the refrigerator. Thinks her husband doesn't transfer energy properly on the backswing. Rumored to have had affair with the club pro two years ago, but denies it, somewhat weakly. Pastel City.

SPECIAL GOLF SKILLS: Makes chip shots Juli Inkster couldn't make in her dreams. Drives 250, average. Secretly plays for big dough on Tuesdays, never ever loses, except once in 1986 when the family had to sell their house to pay up.
HANDICAP: 6
GOLF HERO: Fred Couples' ex-wife.
GOLF QUOTE: "I can't drive the kids to school, I've got a 7:30 tee time."

The Kind of Commercials on During Golf Tournaments

You're watching a PGA golf tournament. You're an average wage slave, pretty much like everyone else in the United States, with the same prole tastes in consumer products. Suddenly, just after you've watched Couples putt out, there's a commercial for General Dynamics' exciting new F-18. Sure, you'd like to take one of those little hummers out for a test drive—maybe Kelly McGillis could show you how, but the missus would never . . . wait a minute.

What the hell is an ad for an F-18 doing on TV? Well, it's not meant for you, Mr. Two Car, 2.2 Kids, and Large MasterCard Balance. It's meant for that Captain of Industry who is watching that very same golf tournament in his 8,900 square foot teak-and-marble palace while you're sucking down the Cheetos in your tract house. Let's look at a typical advertising commercial sequence during a televised tournament.

"Oh, nice drive by Norman . . . about 280, maybe 290 . . . nice hand for the Great White Shark . . . we'll be back after this . . . NATIONAL DEFENSE IS LIKE A TOUGH LIE . . . YOU'VE GOT TO HAVE THE RIGHT EQUIPMENT AND TALENT TO GET OUT OF ROUGH SITUATIONS . . . THE DEATHBLADE CLOSE AIR COVER CHOPPER BY BELL LETS YOU FLY OFF THE TEE INTO THE FRIENDLY FAIRWAYS OF SECURITY . . . BELL HELICOPTERS—WHEN YOU NEED TO REALLY TAKE A SWING WITH FIREPOWER. Back to 16 . . . Strange is lying about 175 from the pin . . . he bogeyed on 15 and he needs a good shot here to stay in the hunt . . . takes a good cut, and puts it right on the fringe . . . can't be happy with that shot . . . more after this . . . THE PEACEKEEPER MISSILE . . . RIGHT FOR YOU . . . RIGHT FOR THE COUNTRY . . . JOHN DALY SAYS, "WHEN THIS COUNTRY NEEDS A LONG SHOT, ROCKWELL IS THERE WITH AN ICBM WITH LOFT AND VELOCITY." THE PEACEKEEPER—OUR ACE IN THE HOLE. Let's go to Byron Nelson on 17 . . ."

All-Purpose Golf Joke Punchline Roundup

Golf jokes are so unremittingly stupid, and yet they are told over and over again by linkster wits. In the interest of eliminating the middleman, the top 25 golf punchlines are presented below, in the hopes of stopping this insidious alleged humor genre dead in its tracks.

1. "I said, 'Putting green, not Lorne Greene.'"
2. "That's no lady, that's my caddy in drag."
3. "That's my shank, buddy, not yours."
4. "Your Mashie Niblick, Madame."
5. "I've got your six iron . . . right here."
6. "I thought you said 'stroke.'"
7. "Your balls or mine?"
8. "I've got the chip if you've got the shot."
9. "Picture window? What picture window?"
10. "He's playing about two clubs short of a regulation bag."
11. "Ping! Ping! Ping!"
12. "I said, 'Play a round.'"
13. "Now that's addressing the ball."
14. "Graphite shaft? More like rubber."
15. "Nice placement."
16. "Hooked it again, dear."
17. "So he said, 'I thought I got a green jacket.'"
18. "Wood or metal? I'm not into that sort of thing."
19. "Okay, here's your downhill lie."
20. "She had sand in her trap."
21. "Rough? My good woman, that was gentle."
22. "Oh yeah? Well, I went to the John Daly party, too."
23. "Just pretend it's a divot."
24. "There's no lie like a bad lie."
25. "What club speed problem?"

How to Improve Your Lie

Lying, unfortunately, is an integral component of the game of golf. And, frankly, it may become necessary not only to fabricate from time to time, but to tell flatly, bald-facedly, and unashamedly the greatest prevarication of the twentieth century.

You can do it.

Why do you have to lie, and what do you have to lie about?

First, you must lie about your score. It's a given. It's etched in stone, an article of faith, and a central tenet of being a linkster. There are simply too many overwhelmingly embarrassing moments in golf scoring not to lie. But, as in life, there are degrees of permissible lying. Let us explore those.

THE FUDGE—A Fudge would be considered shaving a stroke off your performance on any given hole. It would be socially acceptable to permit, say, three Fudges per game. When do you Fudge? It is considered very unsporting to Fudge a score down from five strokes on a hole down to four to achieve par. That's outside the bounds of decency, really. Take the bogey like a man. Unless it's match play, of course. An acceptable Fudge would be useful in the circumstance of shooting a, gulp, ten on a hole, but taking a nine. At that point, who cares? You're out of the game anyway. Some cases may permit going from a nine to an eight or even to a seven if you're playing with relatives.

THE UNTRUE ASSERTION—The Untrue Assertion would be invoked in a situation where you swung at a ball and missed completely. You would then say, at room conversational volume level, "Practice swing." Nobody's going to say a thing. Another Untrue Assertion scenario would be when you hit a shot into the rough, lost your ball, but found another ball that was playable on the edge of the rough; you would then forget about your original ball and announce, "Oh, here it is." No penalty, but be careful not to tee off with a white ball and then play a yellow or orange ball out of the rough. That's tacky.

THE FLAT-OUT FALSEHOOD—The Flat-Out Falsehood is not a capital crime but must be

used extremely judiciously to avoid the accusation that you are indeed lying. Avoid getting caught at all costs. You may use the Flat-Out Falsehood when you have five putted but wish to say you four putted. You may also use the Flat-Out Falsehood by moving loose materials away from your ball. Everybody does that. You may also kick the ball just far enough so that you don't have to buy a new five iron if you wrap it around a tree. Be stealthy, however.

THE CREDIBLE WHOPPER—The Credible Whopper is invoked when you are describing your game to friends and acquaintances after the round is completed, particularly in the pro shop. You may, for example, say, "I hit a six iron shot 200 yards and was two feet from the pin," because that has been known to happen. Mostly on the Tour, by people who earn in the low seven figures playing golf, but still, lightning does strike. An Incredible Whopper would be along the lines of, "I teed off on the 501-yard par five with a seven iron, used the wrong end of a putter for my approach shot, and chipped out of the bunker with a fairway wood into the cup, which was 51 yards from the fringe." Remember, and this is not an oxymoron: Lie credibly.

THE PATHOLOGICAL LIE—The Pathological Lie is for those poor sick souls who must overemphasize every single element of their game. Certain statements are dead giveaways:

"I was talking to Arnie about the grip problem, and he said maybe rubbing a little Pennzoil on the shaft might reduce aerodynamic drag."

"My Master's Jacket is at the cleaners."

"I told Harvey Penick to just shut the hell up."

Presidential Golf Games

Many of our former presidents have been golfers. Some have been better golfers than presidents, and vice versa. It is far preferable, if you seek national elective office, to serve as vice president if you wish to enhance your golf game. For instance, former Vice President Dan Quayle, by all accounts a real nice guy but clearly the junior partner in the Bush–Quayle relationship, could and did blow President Bush's doors off on the links. He had a 6 handicap, and his own wife said that "everybody knows Dan would rather play golf than have sex." In contrast, President Bush's game was never fully reported in our nation's media, other than remarking about how fast he played. Pundits referred to his game as "aerobic golf." Of course, to the national press corps, walking over to the coffee machine counts as reaching a peak heart rate. So let's rate Presidential Golf Games:

PRESIDENT BILL CLINTON—Clinton is an enthusiastic golfer. He golfs often and chews a large unlit cigar while playing. His score is never reported, and in fact, he once berated an aide because cameras got too close to him while he was playing. He is said to have a really good drive and a spotty short game. He wears downscale Democratic tacky sweatshirts and team logo caps while playing to let his constituency know he thinks it's wrong for people to have $750,000 homes on golf courses.

PRESIDENT BUSH—Bush was a rabid golfer at his home in Kennebunkport but was at heart a fisherman. You can't really be good at both, just because of the financial drain, but he tried. Bush would tear around in a golf cart and finish 18 holes in two hours, barely leaving the cart to swing. No scores have ever been reported, but it's probably safe to say he shoots in the 80s.

CLINTON

BUSH

PRESIDENT RONALD REAGAN—Reagan golfed exactly once a year at the Augusta National course, with George Shultz and Caspar Weinberger and some other California wheel. You can probably imagine how good his score was. Reporters were barred from the state of Georgia during his game and martial law was invoked to enforce it.

REAGAN

I ONCE PLAYED BOBBY JONES IN A 1936 WARNER BROS. FILM...

PRESIDENT JIMMY CARTER—Carter never golfed. He fly fished, which is the evil twin of golf, so he gets points there.

PRESIDENT GERALD FORD—Ford was an excellent golfer who shot in the 70s. He once hit someone on the head with a ball while golfing as vice president, as did former Vice President Spiro Agnew. Must have been a Watergate influence of some kind. Ford now lives on a golf course. Enough said.

PRESIDENT RICHARD NIXON—Described by *LIFE* magazine as an "earnest but determined" golfer, Nixon shot in the nineties. He had a workman-like swing and, as vice president, was often photographed with Ike while both men wore polo shirts and pants pulled up to their nipples. If he didn't lie about his score, it would be somewhat out of character, shall we say.

PRESIDENT LYNDON JOHNSON—Johnson never golfed. Johnson shot deer on his ranch and laughed after he did it. This is an entirely different meaning to a hole in one.

PRESIDENT JOHN F. KENNEDY—Kennedy was a very good golfer. He golfed all his life and, according to biographers, went to great lengths to conceal his love of the game due to his image of youth and vigor, in contrast with the golf-happy Halcion Eisenhower Golf Epoch.

PRESIDENT DWIGHT EISENHOWER—Indeed, the president most associated with golf was Ike. He may well have established a sort of national golf metaphor for the '50s: kind of slow but steady and predictable, no fast action, just green grass and blue skies. Ike was a good golfer and provided cartoonists with an inexhaustible supply of golfing imagery. Played at Burning Tree and prevented a nuclear war from the 13th hole. Okay, maybe that's apocryphal.

PRESIDENT ABRAHAM LINCOLN—Lincoln, a fanatical golfer, played so often that wags coined the term "Linkster" after his obsessive play during the Civil War. Invaded Georgia so he could play at Augusta.

Settling Old Scores

Everyone's familiar with the names for the number of strokes it takes to get into the hole, but a new set of names has been developed above triple bogey. Included with the established names, they are:

TWO UNDER: Eagle
ONE UNDER: Birdie
EVEN: Par
ONE OVER: Bogey
TWO OVER: Double Bogey
THREE OVER: Triple Bogey
FOUR OVER: Bogey and Bacall
FIVE OVER: Jesus

SIX OVER: Jesus, Mary, and Joseph
SEVEN OVER: Oh my God
EIGHT OVER: I quit this goddamned game forever
NINE OVER: Do you want to buy my clubs?
TEN OVER: I'll give you my clubs
ELEVEN OVER: Whimper
TWELVE OVER: AAAAAAAAAAAIIIIIIIIIIIIIIEEEEEEEEE-EEE!!!!!!!!!!!!!!
THIRTEEN OVER: GGGGGRRRRRRRRRRRAAAAAUUUUU-UGGGGGGGGHHHHHNNN
FOURTEEN OVER: URKKKKGGGGGGLLLLLLLEEEE
FIFTEEN OVER: SNNNNLLLLLLLL
SIXTEEN OVER: ——————————————————————
(flatline)

Is Golf Exercise?

Many people take up golf because they are under the delusion that golf is exercise. It is an exercise, but is not, technically, exercise. Okay, maybe it is, in the sense that stock car drivers are often referred to as athletes. But in order to be considered true exercise in the cardiovascular, physiological sense, one must elevate one's heart rate. How to combine golf with actual exercise is a topic that was examined at the National Exercise Sports Physiology Data Center in Ames, Iowa. Scientists made the following observations and recommendations to ensure that each round of golf isn't just a pleasant diversion but a full-blown cardiovascular workout:

1. CARRY YOUR CART. Carrying your golf cart, according to the study, burns approximately 2300 calories per hour, at an ambient daytime temperature of 72 degrees Fahrenheit. Be sure to use your knees instead of your back when picking the cart up to avoid needless injury.

2. BAD GOLFERS ARE HEALTHY GOLFERS. The study showed that golfers who made more than 170 swings per round were toning crucial upper body muscles and providing rhythmic arm motion, which are critical in reaching peak aerobic benefit. One hundred seventy swings were determined to be near-constant arm motion.

3. PRIMAL SCREAMS ARE GOOD FOR YOU. If a golfer emitted more than 50 primal screams per hour in reaction to poor play, this was determined to be sufficient lung exercise to reach target heart rates. In addition, emitting primal screams releases endorphins and relieves inner tension, which are always beneficial to overall health and mental well-being.

4. HIT EVERYONE'S BALL. If a golfer took the initiative of hitting everyone's ball in a bogey-shooting foursome, while maintaining an eight minute per mile pace, excellent health benefits would be realized. The downside is that the golfer performing this activity may well be seriously injured by his partners.

TARGET
HEART
RATE
ESTABLISHED
AT A
SCORE OF
170
SWINGS
PER
ROUND

PRIMAL
SCREAM
THERAPY:
CATHARTIC, AEROBIC

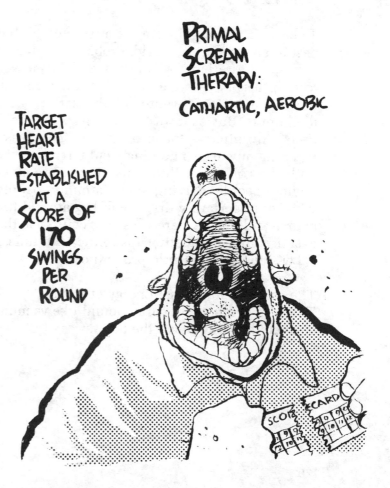

Carts

To be sure, golf carts were invented with all the best intentions in the world. Probably originally conceived as a labor-saving device, or as a way to help less-mobile golfers still enjoy a round, the intent of the inventor of the cart was no doubt pure. But, as it was with many well-intentioned inventions—tobacco, nuclear power, easy listening music—something went terribly awry with the golf carts. Suddenly, there were able-bodied people driving them around; people who could certainly drag a golf bag around the course and maybe, dare we say it, could use the exercise after too many trips to the 19th hole.

Let's engage in a little pro and con:

The case for golf carts: Energy efficient
The case against golf carts: Sound like vacuum cleaners heading down the fairway.

The case for golf carts: Helps slow people golf
The case against golf carts: Helps slow people golf

The case for golf carts: Gives you a place to put your beer
The case against golf carts: Puts more drunks on the course

The case for golf carts: Creates jobs
The case against golf carts: So does nuclear waste

Home on the Range

In between our rounds of golf, we must find a way to keep our game and hitting prowess in top form. In a stunning market stroke of genius, the driving range was invented. The overhead on a driving range is next to zero: just lease a piece of worthless farmland, buy crummy balls by the metric ton, and you're in business.

While at the driving range, you should note the following immutable laws:

1. Your average drive is 110 yards further on a driving range than your average drive at the golf course. Drives at the range are invariably straight, due to a magnetic homing device set at the far side of the range itself.

2. You will always be driving next to someone who emits loud, bellowing snorts and grunts and is working on a ten-inch Macanudo cigar at the same time.

3. Amazingly, cut balls fly just as far as regular, expensive "get 20 extra yards" balls that you've purchased for 20 bucks per box.

4. You will, at least once during a practice session, hit your ball basket.

5. Rubber practice tees are virtually useless and are there to ensure you buy another bucket of balls.

6. Tees will appear to be quietly reproducing in the grass immediately in front of your position if you're not using a rubber tee. Leave them alone; these are tee spawning beds, and this is where tees come from.

7. Just as someone walks by, even if you've been hammering them like John Daly all day, your ball will only travel a short distance and bounce harmlessly off the 50 yard marker sign. This will elicit a low chuckle from the walker, further putting you off your swing.

How to Choose a Golf Ball

The golf ball is one of the true mysteries of the game. It's denser than a teaspoonful of the sun, and yet it can fly through the air with ease, given the proper swing. One golf ball is seemingly like all the others, so how does one tell a good one from a bad one?

The first sign is price, of course. The more expensive the ball, the better it is in your own mind. The fact is, with the exception of how well designed the manufacturer's logo is, one ball is virtually indistinguishable from the next.

Personalized golf balls with your name engraved on the cover are known to add five strokes to your game, and offer the casual observer the opportunity to walk up and say with authority and precision just exactly who made such an atrocious shot. That's unacceptable, of course.

Another way to tell a good golf ball from a bad one is if the ball has a corporation logo or insignia on it. Balls that have logos such as Rockwell International, Xerox, or Paine Webber are probably of higher quality than those balls with logos from Buck and Candi's Pancake House or Exhaust Breath Eddie's House o' Mufflers.

One of the great urban folklore rumors of all time revolves around the contents of the center of a golf ball. It has been firmly established that there is, in fact, no acid in the center of the average ball. However, in 1993, the Consumer Product Safety Council conducted an exhaustive six-year effort to determine just what, exactly, *was* in the center of a golf ball. The results are preliminary, but traces of Jimmy Hoffa were found in several test drilling core samples.

Things to look for in a bad ball:

- Shaped like a football, brown, and made of leather.
- Has a little pupil and iris staring up at you.
- Appears to be a potato.
- Has a light covering of flour instead of paint.
- Has the name of a law enforcement agency stenciled on the cover.

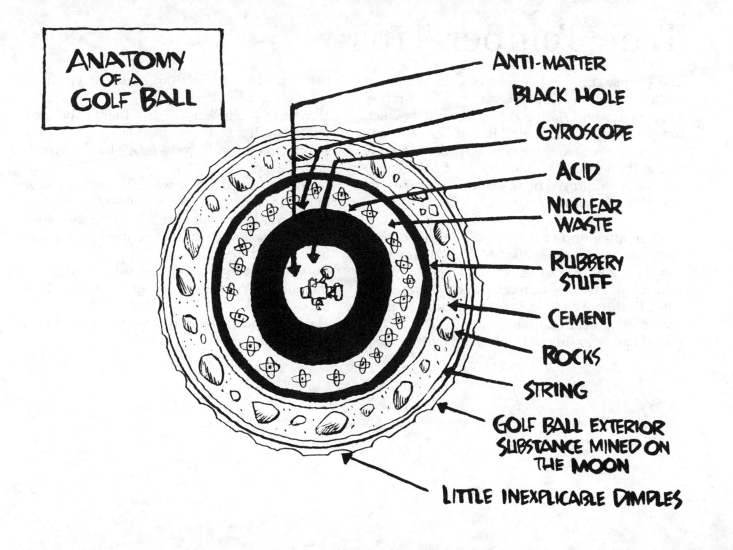

ANATOMY OF A GOLF BALL

ANTI-MATTER

BLACK HOLE

GYROSCOPE

ACID

NUCLEAR WASTE

RUBBERY STUFF

CEMENT

ROCKS

STRING

GOLF BALL EXTERIOR SUBSTANCE MINED ON THE MOON

LITTLE INEXPLICABLE DIMPLES

True Temper Tips

The proper throwing of a fit is a time-honored golfing tradition. And yet, many golfers refuse to observe some simple rules of etiquette when blowing their stack. This kind of behavior can get you booted from some of our nation's truly fine golf courses. These methods of losing your temper are approved by the USGA as well as the American Heart Association.

• When attempting to roll your golf cart over in a fit of pique, remember to always use your legs instead of your back.

• Irons should be thrown directly over your head, while woods and putters should be flung with a sidearm motion.

• Golf balls should not be eaten unless the cover has a previously existing crack to ensure a good incisor hold.

• Don't use a club any higher than a five iron when chasing your opponents.

• Divots made with your face should always be replaced.

• Don't pull up the ball washers unless you've muffed five consecutive tee shots.

• Don't ever throw your club bag into the water. Some bags have lead-based dyes and could harm wildlife.

• You may not legally commit suicide while on the course. Wait until you get to the parking lot.

• Don't ask the marshal to arrest you to end your round because of poor play.

Unreliable Golf Clubs

1. Ping Zippos
2. The Playful Kitten Drivers by Lynx
3. CrystalShafts by Steuben Glass
4. Pro Staff Balsaheads
5. Limp Shaft 2000s
6. I Can't Believe It's a Driver and a Putter!
7. Chunka-Tins
8. Melted Down Sinkers Customs
9. RubberWoods by Goodyear
10. Scrap Metal Woods by Reynolds Aluminum

Unreliable Golf Balls

1. Titleist EggShell XL
2. Pinnacle Acid Core
3. Top-Flite LeadBall Express
4. The Dimple Master
5. Wilson Quartzball
6. Range Ball Minus
7. Dog Chewed 6
8. Kinda Oval by Spaulding
9. Liquid Cherry Centers by Whitman
10. Fuzzy Green Tennis-like Golf Balls

Mulligan

A question that often arises during play is when to exercise your option of taking a Mulligan. A Mulligan, of course, is that free stroke the golf gods determined you may have if you make some sort of unpardonable shot. Amongst certain golfers, a Mulligan seems to be taken every hole, so you may want to consult your local foursome for their peculiar Mulligan rules. However, the generally accepted practice is to take one Mulligan on the front nine and one Mulligan on the back nine.

How do you know just when to take Mulligan? It's easy to determine if you memorize this simple list of Mulligan Guidelines.

Take a Mulligan if you've just killed your partner with a tee shot.

Take a Mulligan if you've hit a drive backwards into the pro shop picture window.

Take a Mulligan if you're about waist deep in a water hazard and there's an alligator longer than ten feet swimming in your approximate direction.

Take a Mulligan if a shot has traveled less than three feet.

Take a Mulligan if no one will catch you, just on general principle.

Take a Mulligan if your blood pressure after a shot is above 160/100.

Take a Mulligan if you think it will help you win the Masters.

How to Compute Your Handicap

Perhaps the first thing a fellow golfer will ask you about is your handicap. If you're not terribly proficient at golf, it's almost like being asked how many people you've slept with in the last ten years. A low number in this day and age is probably the best number. The question is, however, just how does one compute one's own handicap?

Well, it's easy once you learn a few simple shortcuts.

TAKE YOUR AVERAGE SCORE AND SHAVE OFF 20 STROKES. This will provide a base number for you to work with that isn't socially debilitating. Twenty strokes turns a below-average golfer into an acceptable golfer, or at least one that can be brought around the club without losing your place in the Social Register.

TAKE THAT NUMBER AND KNOCK OFF TEN MORE STROKES. What the hell. It's only a game.

TAKE THE NUMBER 72 AND MULTIPLY IT BY 3.1416. This will give you the circumference of the golf hole.

SUBTRACT YOUR AVERAGE SCORE MINUS 30 STROKES FROM THE SQUARE ROOT OF THE NUMBER OF GOLF CARTS AT PEBBLE BEACH. Self-explanatory, really.

TAKE THE AVERAGE ANNUAL INCOME OF ALL THE CADDIES AT YOUR CLUB, INVERT THE MULTIPLIER, AND SUBVERT THE TUTORIAL FRANGIBLE NUMBER BY ITS HYPOTENUSE. This will convert your handicap into a respectable number: 6.

$\sqrt{\text{INFIELD FLY RULE}}$ (NUMBER OF DIVOTS IN VERMONT) $\dfrac{[\text{TEES IN YOUR PARTNER'S GOLF BAG}] \times}{(\text{NUMBER OF BALLS IN WATER HAZARDS IN SCOTLAND}) \sqrt{\text{SPIKE MARKS MADE BY EISENHOWER}} \, (\pi)}$

[1936 CLEVELAND INDIANS SLUGGING AVERAGE] {BYRON NELSON ON 17} (∞)

(DISTANCE OF 16th HOLE AT PEBBLE BEACH IN METERS) [CUBE ROOT OF NUMBER OF EMPTY BALL PACKAGES IN YOUR GOLF BAG) + (YOUR SCORE ON JULY 8th, 1993 + YOUR WIFE'S AVERAGE WEIGHT − YOUR LAST THREE MINIATURE GOLF SCORES + THE POPULATION (1990 CENSUS) OF COLUMBUS, OHIO + ARNOLD PALMER'S NET INCOME + GROSS DEPRECIATION OF 1974 PLYMOUTHS IN RUBLES × THE AVERAGE ANNUAL RAINFALL OF PARAGUAY IN TEASPOONS × YOUR AVERAGE DISTANCE WITH A SIX IRON + WHO IS BURIED IN GRANT'S TOMB)

= 9 HANDICAP

HANDICAP COMPUTATION DESK

3   1

USGA

Rain Play

As hardy golfers, there comes a time when the elements must be dealt with. Usually, the urge to golf immediately follows a prolonged beer and snack food sit-down in front of the TV watching a major golf tournament played in nice weather. But, as you look outside, you remember that you do not, unfortunately, live in a tropical area and decide to go golfing anyway. Since golf tournaments are shown on weekends, you will make this decision on a weekend, and it being a weekend, it will be raining. In this case, you will have to deal with this eventuality.

Golfing in the rain is not as bad as it sounds. Thoughtful golf equipment manufacturers have developed state-of-the-art golf rainwear that is only about as restrictive as an Apollo spacesuit. Umbrellas the size of radar dishes—particularly useful and aerodynamic in high winds—have been invented, mostly to display a large eye-grabbing logo. And, of course, there are the 4 × 4 golf carts. Certain rain rules have been developed and are pending before the USGA. They are:

1. Any water that a golfer has accidentally drowned in can be defined as casual water.

2. Any golfer killed by lightning is entitled to a 50 percent refund of his or her green fee.

3. Fellow golfers may not guffaw more than one minute at the sight of a fellow golfer in a translucent rain suit.

4. At the first sight of lightning, slow-moving foursomes who have consistently delayed play all day must head for a very tall tree and hold their nine irons high above their heads.

5. Water-saturated divots weighing more than ten pounds must be replaced with a backhoe.

6. A golfer who slips on a downhill lie and slides on his fanny for more than 100 feet will be assessed a two-stroke penalty.

7. Water running down your back may not be defined as casual water.

8. Water-saturated grips causing the club to fly out of one's hands during a swing will be blamed as a cause but not an excuse for the action cited. Every golfer within sight is allowed two derisive comments of ten words or fewer.

9. Ducks or geese swimming in your bag are assessed a one-stroke penalty.

10. Flowing duck or goose poop is not allowable as "casual water."

Winter Rules

Winter Rules are often conveniently invoked, say, after the Fourth of July, usually by older players who are, technically, in the winter of their lives. Younger players who wish to play golf on the up and up will have to confine their invocation of Winter Rules from the period beginning on the winter solstice and ending on the vernal equinox.

Winter Rules means taking some latitude, shall we say, with ball placement. Normally, the ball should be played where it lies; that generally means that it's inconveniently located to begin with, like in dense foliage or squarely behind a tree or under a large tractor. In the summer, that's just tough tees, pal. But under the marvel of Winter Rules, ball placement and "impediments" can be dealt with in an extremely civilized manner: They can be disposed of entirely.

Winter Rules—in the winter or otherwise—are an option only under the following conditions:

1. The ball won't fly to the hole in a straight line unless the John Deere is moved.
2. The ball is lost in a glacier field.
3. The ball is lost in Alaska.
4. The ball is within seven statute miles of a refrigerator.
5. The ball is covered with an unidentified but strongly suspect brown pasty substance.
6. The ball is wedged in someone's incisors.
7. The ball is balanced on top of the pin.
8. The ball didn't go where you wanted it to go.
9. The ball is under a large, frightening animal.
10. The ball is on fire.
11. The ball has been dipped in liquid nitrogen and molecular motion has ceased.

ABOUT THE AUTHOR

Jack Ohman was born on September 1, 1960, very near a municipal golf course in St. Paul, Minnesota. He is the editorial cartoonist for *The Oregonian*, and his work is syndicated in 150 newspapers across the United States. He is the father of two children: Eric, born in 1988, and Julia, born in 1991. He owns a set of Mizuno clubs and two Ping putters. Ohman is said to be a convivial golf partner, except after a triple bogey.